THE PAIN I ENDURED

One woman's story
of overcoming
religious abuse

Jessica Beckum

The Pain I Endured

One woman's story of overcoming religious abuse

Jessica Beckum

T&J Publishers

A SMALL INDEPENDENT PUBLISHER WITH A BIG VOICE

Printed in the United States of America by
T&J Publishers (Atlanta, GA.)
www.TandJPublishers.com

© Copyright 2020 by Jessica Beckum

All rights reserved. This book or parts thereof may not be reproduced in any form, stored in a retrieval system, or transmitted in any form by any means-electronic, mechanical, photocopy, recording, or otherwise-without prior written permission of the author, except as provided by United States of America copyright law.

Cover Design by Timothy Flemming, Jr. (T&J Publishers)
Book Format/Layout by Timothy Flemming, Jr.

ISBN: 978-1-7345105-8-4

To contact the author, go to:
J.Beckum1117@icloud.com

To my two beautiful children, Conner Beckum and Paisley Beckum if life brings you to walk in these shoes, this book is your guide.

"Nay, in all these things we are more than conquerors through him that loved us."
—Romans 8:37

TABLE OF CONTENTS

Where It All Begin	11
The Endurance	23
The Choice	33
Closure	37
I Thought I Was Over It	45
I Overcame	53

Chapter One
WHERE IT ALL BEGAN

> The definition of "hurt" is *"to cause physical pain or injury to."* The experience of hurt in general is painful, and quite frankly, it could be **traumatizing**. Hurt caused by **anyone** can be hard to deal with, but most people would say **church hurt is the worse kind**. That's the experience I would like to share with you in the pages of this book.

July 2014 was the day I felt compelled to join a new church. My heart was full, and my spirit refreshed. I was excited about a fresh start, about God taking me to a higher destination. I immediately joined the youth praise team when I joined that ministry. I was happy about meeting new people; in fact, we were all excited; this was a new experience for all of us.

As we'd lead praise and worship, people would come from near and far. Youth Sundays were the best - people would pack the church out. As the months went by, the devil crept in. He was angry that we were doing such a great thing for the glory of God. Suddenly, a division arose, and conflict broke out between the team members. One member grew jealous and upset with the other members, and things started to get heated. Members began spreading lies on one another, and everyone was turning against each other. We discovered that one of the team members went to the church's leaders secretly and began telling them lies about what was going on.

Of course, the devil was mad. Why wouldn't he be? We were doing so well at first, touching so many lives for the Kingdom of God. And now, so much chaos and confusion were taking place. But I felt we couldn't give the enemy what he wanted. Eventually, the church's leader came to talk to us. We were sure that he would see the situation through a spiritual lens and recognize that the devil was behind this mess and squash it, but that's not what happened. We thought he'd be glad to see us, young girls, in the ministry, discovering our paths, and drawing so many young people to Christ. Sadly, the church's leader didn't see our potential and the work we'd done for Christ, and he resorted to bashing us,

CHAPTER 1: WHERE IT ALL BEGAN

disrespecting us, and even ridiculing us. And for what? All because of rumors and lies. He was going off of one side of the story, and he made a bad judgment call without taking into account the full story. This crushed me. I remember my heart was pounding, my head was aching, and my eyes were burning from crying so much. I had never experienced such harsh treatment from anyone, let alone from a leader in the church. However, as time went by, things settled down, and we were back to doing what we did best: singing to the glory of God.

Fast forward, God was about to promote me yet again. I had met the man of my life, and we got engaged. Around this time, the church's leadership asked me to join the main praise team. Although I knew this day was coming because God had already spoken to me about it, revealing that he was going to further develop my gift in this area, when the promotion came, I was excited. The first year, I was learning the routine of praise and worship. I was fresh and new, so I wanted to get the hang of things before I tried to lead any songs. Everything was going smooth. I prayed and asked God to give me a unique way to lead worship. I wanted God to shape and mold me as he saw fit. I also sought help and advice from the other team members.

As a team, I believed we would look out for one another and help each other along the way. I especially thought they'd help a young girl like me since they were the veterans in the group. It didn't take me long to find out that things aren't always what they seem. Several of the team members greeted me with jealousy, stupidity, and ignorance. You wouldn't think that the veterans - the ones who had been doing this for years - would be intimidated by a fresh, young girl with a unique sound and style. You'd think they'd be happy, considering that it's all for the glory of God. Unfortunately, backstabbing, backbiting, malice, and deceit laid the foundation for the team. As time went by, two-years to be exact, I noticed that they were overlooking me. Not once had I been asked to lead praise and worship. They were happy to keep me in the background. Even still, I was content with being just a background singer. I wasn't hungry for a spotlight, but I also knew there was more God wanted me to do, and that I needed to use my gift to the fullest. Despite all of this, I didn't complain; I stayed faithful.

One night, while sitting in my front room, a message popped up on my phone; one of the praise team members mistakenly sent me the message about secret rehearsals that were taking place outside of the regular rehearsals - one with only specific team members. Of course, this was confusing to me. One of my sisters called and said, "Hey, girl, did you see the message that just popped up?" I said,

"Yes. I wonder what's that about because we haven't had any practices lately." Before we knew it, the team member wrote back and said that they created another praise team for the church's annual conference. A certain higher-up needed singers for the conference - they chose not to give me a spot on that team or even

CHAPTER 1: WHERE IT ALL BEGAN

tell me about it. My heart dropped into my stomach. The feeling of rejection felt like someone hit me in the gut and knocked the wind out my body. I just sat still on the couch, feeling devastated. The church leaders later called for the entire praise team to discuss the matter. I remember driving in my car, hoping and praying that this wasn't what it was. I was hoping that the leaders were making changes, better ones. Once I arrived at the meeting, the main leader was standing there. Once the meeting started, he told us that they'd decided to go with a different look and sound for the conference. The room was silent. All I could do was keep my head down, swallow my tears, and try to keep a straight face. I was disappointed. *Don't they see my faithfulness?* I thought to myself. *I put my heart and soul into this ministry, serving with a sincere heart, and apparently, that means nothing to them.* After the meeting, I approached one of the team members that made the cut and asked, "So, why wasn't I picked?" They answered,

"Because your worship isn't as broad as ours. You look like you're in La-La Land, which makes you immature. Your facial expressions aren't together, and we just felt like you weren't a good fit; this wasn't just my decision; it came from the first family down to the church. We all agreed." Once again, that messed me up. I didn't look like everyone else, and that's why they skipped over me. I knew that their attitude and response wasn't consistent with God's will and character. They were rude. Yes, I wanted them to include me on the team; I also wanted everyone to like me and treat me as an equal. I just wanted to be accepted and not be considered the oddball for once. That ride home seemed so long. I kept thinking, crying and believing that this could turn around for me, but it didn't.

As time went by, I became insecure and felt unworthy and unwanted. I asked God why did he bless me with such a gift and why nobody wanted to use me? Eventually, my time came, and the team leader asked me to lead praise and worship. I will never forget that moment. All week, I prayed and prepared myself for praise and worship. When I got to the church, and worship began, it was my turn to lead worship. I prayed before I began to sing. And then, I immediately looked at the people in the audience and noticed that they were acting cold towards me. They'd grown used to hearing *certain* voices, and mine was not one of them. The moment I touched the mic, I could see deaf ears turning. I became intimidated by the people, and even by the other team members. I began putting myself down. I felt like my gift was useless. I felt worthless. But I didn't give up; instead, I just kept crying and praying my way through. I was always told not to let people see you sweat, so I held it together.

During my hopeless state, God prompted me to become a handmaiden - could you say a double dose of warfare? I was faithful to the praise team, even while being faithful to my job as a handmaiden. Being a handmaiden wasn't peaches and cream. You could feel attacks coming from other sisters who were jealous

CHAPTER 1: WHERE IT ALL BEGAN

because they didn't want you to serve better than them. I remember someone telling me there aren't any "I"'s in "team" but I believe some of these sisters didn't understand the definition of "team". I would serve when nobody wanted to. I served after I finished singing, I served, even alone. I served when I didn't feel like it. Once the annual conference came, I found myself at the back door greeting visitors. Now let me say this: Anything you do for Christ will last. I did this wholeheartedly. I had two positions that I was faithful to at this church, but I always found myself just not good enough when it came down to this conference. I know you're saying, "So one conference can make you feel that way about yourself?" Yes. How would you feel if you were practicing all year for the playoffs and when game day came coach didn't let you play? All that hard work and time you put in just for them to overlook you and put others before you. I would see people who didn't attend my church singing on the praise team during the conference and leading songs - it took me two years just to lead a song. I would see women serving who weren't even faithful coming to the church; they were inexperienced and simply wanted a limelight during the conference. My heart broke. And yet, I stayed committed.

    I kept coming, praying, and tithing, even though, at times, I'd be out of work. I found ways to tithe with no money. Yes, I said "with no money" and while behind on bills. I had food stamps, so I would make sure that whatever the church lacked, from water to peppermints, I would furnish. During revivals, I would give my last.

17

Sometimes, I had to choose between eating or getting gas, but since I didn't want my church to suffer, I'd skip a meal. I was there, faithful with a whole heart.

Another year went by, and honestly, things were beginning to look up for me. I stayed in prayer. I remember asking God to reward not only my faithfulness but everyone who had been faithful in ministry despite being treated like underdogs. I prayed for God to help us to operate with the right spirit: not hungry to be seen, but to glorify God. Things began to come together. Finally, I was able to operate in my position. Of course, the fight didn't stop. I still felt pressured to prove myself. I was still trying to prove that I could operate under pressure, under any circumstance; that my age was not a hindrance.

I didn't have the same relationship with the church's leaders as many of the seasoned team members, so it seemed like I had so much pressure on me; it seemed like I was the only one who had to prove myself. It didn't matter what I did; the leaders would always place other people ahead of me. I was rarely a pick, and if I were, the leaders would always make sure to remind me to be grateful to have a spot. They would make it clear that they could fire me and place someone else in my spot at any time. I realized that I could lose everything I'd worked for in a moment. And it was indeed a challenge for me. I had to deal with situations where, for example, there was one lady who didn't like the fact that I was in the position that I was and wanted to bring me down.

CHAPTER 1: WHERE IT ALL BEGAN

My husband and I both experienced people plotting against us out of jealousy. I had members come up to me and say things that were out of the way. In every case, I knew I was under the microscope and had to conduct myself in a particular manner since "certain" people were anxious to demote me. All they needed was a reason. I knew that if I messed up, I'd become the talk of the entire church. They'd claim that my season was up. None of them would be concerned with the mistreatment I endured.

I had no one to turn to for help. If I presented a problem to the leaders, it would get brushed off, leaving me to deal with the issue on my own. I felt like they were violating my innocence and taking away my voice. There's a saying in the church: "Don't leave out the same way you came in." However, many days I'd leave out of the church's doors feeling even worse than I did entering the building. I had to shut up to keep what I had; this would only last for so long. One thing I learned is no matter how hard you try to prove yourself and change yourself for the sake of people, none of what you do will change whatever perspective they have of you. You have to live and change for God, not people, and keep your focus on him.

I began to push harder despite the odds being against me. Every time I got hit, I didn't stay down long. I'd pull myself up by my bootstraps and get back into the mix. Yes, it was hard getting up after so many blows, but I wasn't a quitter and ministry was my passion. I wanted to give the world a gift, and that gift was God. Beyond that, when it came down to ministry, I knew someone depended on my testimony; therefore, I couldn't give up. I continued to pray and go to the services and meet all of my requirements. Eventually, I grew exhausted of the cycle. I was in desperate need for a word from the lord. I needed strength; I needed a refreshing; I needed one word. One night after church service, my family and I went home, had dinner, and prepared ourselves for bed. While in bed, I suffered an anxiety attack. I woke up, confused. My mind was rushing. I ran to the bathroom, fell on the floor, rocked back and forth and began praying. Fear gripped on me. I could smell and taste fear; it sat on my tongue; it was bitter. I felt numb. That was something I'd never experienced before. Even today, I can still taste the fear and remember the feeling I felt that night.

    The following Sunday, I returned to the church, anxious for God to speak to me. Our church flowed heavily in the gift of prophecy and words of knowledge. Due to my situation, I expected to receive a word of guidance or encouragement from one of the ministers, but I didn't get one. I prayed and cried out to God, but didn't receive anything from him. I couldn't even feel God. I felt fearful and alone. I was crying out for help in the middle of a room full of people, but nobody could hear me. I found myself singing in fear, serving in fear. Why isn't God speaking to me? Why can't anyone see a difference in me? Months went by I still didn't get a word from God. Prophetic words had become my crutch. If no

CHAPTER 1: WHERE IT ALL BEGAN

one prophesied to me, I believed God wasn't speaking to me. I even thought I was on my way to hell. The anxiety grew, and still no prophetic word. Nevertheless, that didn't stop my commitment to the ministry; it didn't stop my work in the church. I was determined to do the job no matter what because I loved my church, God and my leaders, so nothing held me back.

THE PAIN I ENDURED

Chapter Two
THE ENDURANCE

I know you're wondering *why did you stay for so long?* Why didn't you leave After all those years and many times of mistreatment. My answer to you is I still kept my faith in my leaders and in my church. The worse part is believing in people who don't believe in you but I trusted God. I kept telling myself what was told to me. I wasn't mature enough yet, I had to work my way up, be grateful for where you are everyone wasn't chosen. I believed at that time that was where I suppose to be even if it was just for a season I wanted to give God, my leaders and my church all I had. I was available, on time, faithful, never complained and I really thought that's what God wanted from me. There was nothing my leaders said or done that I went against or didn't believe, if God trusted them so did I.

THE PAIN I ENDURED

So the seasoned changed. The face of the church was changing and so was the sound. The ladies that I started out singing with came over to the regular team and we were the new face of worship. Immediately I knew God was in it. We were all millennials, so I knew what our task was for the time. We begin to come together and do the works but of course before we begin we had to be reminded that we had to be grateful for the position because not everyone was chosen but this time we were told by leadership I see in less time some of y'all won't make it. He made it known that we weren't his pick and if it was his way he would've went another route. Well isn't that encouraging? I remember being in that meeting mad. My heart pounding, my eyes twitching because Once again I was holding tears. Why? Just why can't for once leadership believe in me as much as I believe in them? *Why?* Why is everything so pressured and negative but has a little bible in it to try to make it okay to be mistreated and talk to any kind of way? Once again the pressure was on and we all had to prove ourselves. As time went by here goes the devil. I was attacked by the youth leadership's wife they had included me in their drama. I was completely blind sided. Threats were made toward my family, picking and laughing while we were singing, even in public scandalizing my name and my families. What did we do? I had enough. Was I guilty by association but why is it drama with fellowship? Isn't this church where the people assemble? I had gotten fed up I couldn't take it anymore! Enough was enough. I responded back.

CHAPTER 2: THE ENDURANCE

I couldn't help myself it was like all this build up had taken control. I was more upset about the years of hush then the actual situation. I did what needed to be done. I needed to talk.

I was heated! Everything that I held begin to come out. I couldn't hold anything in any longer, I had been quiet for years. I had taken years of everything I endured being sifted under the rug. I had to be persecuted, I had to be lied on, I had to hear stories that weren't true, I had to lose positions just so other people could look good, everything that I went through always resulted in me looking like the criminal. All of this in the church and coming off the lips of church people. On that day every situation I took and ingurgitated for years had came up like a waterfall, I couldn't stop my hands from shaking, I couldn't stop my thoughts from racing. I wanted to be heard and the more I kept hearing not to respond the more I wanted to burst open with everything I kept on the inside from everyone telling me to hush, to be the bigger person. Why do I always have to be the bigger person? I am always tossed around while everyone says or do what they want. I've been cut and left to bleed while patching other people's wounds and it isn't fair but today was my day. One way or another my voice would be heard even in the worse way. Of course for that very moment it felt so good to express myself, I felt free like all chains and shackles had fallen off my lips, mind, body, and soul. I took a deep breath and for just a minute I felt so good about what I did. Only if that minute would've stuck with me just a little while longer, before I knew it I started feeling bad. I had no business responding, I should have kept my mouth closed. Why did I let her terrorize my character? Everything that was stolen from me all I ever had left was my character now it's gone. I kept beating myself up. We all fall short of the glory, I couldn't stay down long. The Bible says he that knows the way gets whipped with many stripes, so I had to make it right.

After all the conversion and drama cleared up, I had received a phone call from leadership regarding the incident that had just taken place. I was prepared to tell my side of the story which shouldn't be much because I figured since this was ongoing it wouldn't be much to discuss. When I got on the call she begin to play the victim card, immediately it turned from my situation to leadership trying to save their image and becoming selfish. She told me millennials don't listen and how we made the church look bad because so many people were watching them. I was told that I had people blaming leadership for what happened, not once was I told that they understood or how they didn't want for us to leave. I had played by every card they gave me. I was obedient, if they told me to jump I would respond how high. A faithful servant and this is the response I get? I was disturbed, I couldn't believe my ears. How could she play the victim card when I have been dealing with this for years in their ministry and I have reached out on multiple occasions. I decided to do the mature thing and go speak to the senior pastor face to face, maybe I wasn't understanding clearly. The night of the

CHAPTER 2: THE ENDURANCE

meeting I remember praying for peace on my way to the church and for God to just let me be open to whatever I needed to hear and for me to be honest so they could hear my heart. Arriving at the church we all set at the table and I begin to talk and tell my side of the story. I went through the years of how I kept quiet, many times I cried silently and why I exploded the way I did. I asked for forgiveness and told them I would sit down however long I needed and during my time of maternity leave I would get my heart right because so much I had been through I refused to grab a mic with filthy hands and an unforgiving heart. I wanted to assure them that this wouldn't happen again but through the years of me reaching out about all the things that were done, everything had always been swept under the rug and brushed off. I expressed to them how I felt neglected as a sheep. While pouring out my heart I knew leadership would understand but once again it didn't rule in my favor. Leadership told me that I was uncontrollable. I had just opened up a YouTube page because so many people had asked me to do so. I was excited about this new step in life. Leadership told me I seemed thirsty and that nothing should be recorded during praise and worship because it was sacred. He said he couldn't get with this new millennial thing and that he wanted to start over. He didn't want to use the new millennial team. I was torn. I felt like this was all my fault. I left out the meeting hurt, devastated& traumatized. How could you feel this way about someone who you seen sacrifice so much for the ministry? I had a miscarriage twice and was at church singing and serving right out the hospital, my marriage was falling apart but I still sing and served, I left maternity leave at 4 weeks because the praise team had fallen apart, I had money for either gas or food but revival was coming so I used it for gas while they ate, I remember sitting on my bathroom floor trying to come to reality because I was having anxiety attacks so bad I couldn't breathe and I knew I was loosing my mind. I couldn't sleep at night because anxiety would be so heavy but it never stopped me, I stayed in the background looked over, lied on, and never mumbled a word but I stayed faithful, I cried many nights but I never lost my faith in God, leadership or my church. How could he think of me this way? Thirsty? Singing isn't just a gift it's a passion I have.

    The night once again was long. I couldn't understand. I kept trying to check myself to see what or where did I go wrong. I was wondering was I really seeking attention? All I ever wanted was for my gift to touch the hearts of people and they turn to God. I have never been the type to flaunt so where was all this coming from? Did I ever cross him wrong? What about me makes you feel so ill ? So many questions popped in my head with no answers. Days went by and I gave birth to my second child, my baby girl. I was excited to be a mom of two. Boy, did she make me happy. I enjoyed my moment with her but the thoughts of this current situation never ceased. I was still upset and confused but I made sure not to let it get me down. I didn't want my family worried about me so I covered it up, got myself

CHAPTER 2: THE ENDURANCE

together and moved those thoughts to the back of my head. It was New Years morning and the count down was over. I was laying in the hospital bed and I got on my Facebook to see the people's post. So happened I scrolled down my page and I was presented with a flyer from the church where they had a national recording artist became the new praise and worship leader. Once again double crossed, blind sided and in the dark. Was this already planned? Was this entire situation a setup? How did this happen so fast? I immediately put my phone down closed my eyes and shook my head. I had to hold it together my family is here. Lord please give me strength through this.

    Once I got settled in at home, phone calls and messages came. People were asking have I seen the flyer and I told them yes. I eventually got off Facebook for a couple of days until the uproar died but it didn't stop me from hurting. I decided for the first time ever that I would stop going to church. I decided I wasn't going to join anyone church and I would study, read and pray at home. I didn't want no parts all I wanted to do was be happy and have no parts of any church. I don't care what encouraging words was sent to me, I didn't want to hear no scriptures, I didn't want to hear about God I just want to get away, start over and live for my own fleshly needs. For once I wanted to be happy with myself, I wanted 10 more tattoos, I wanted to go to a bar, I wanted to go to a club, I just wanted to rebel. I know your saying well how was that going to solve anything? Well spend your life doing what's right, giving up your dreams for ministry just to get crushed and misused, I guarantee rebellion will be on your mind too. A week went by and Sunday came, I hit up social media and here was the new flyer of the new praise and worship leader. The entire church shared, liked and commented. I couldn't believe it, when we were up nobody supported us. Videos of the services were posted, picture taken. My heart raced because all I could think of was what was told to me. What made her better? Was it her name? Did she have connections, what was it? Before I knew it I broke I wept uncontrollably for hours until my eyes burned and were swollen. I couldn't take it anymore. Lord why me? Why am I catching it so bad? Am I reaping? I begin to pray, all I could tell God was whatever you do don't let me heart turn, don't let me hold a grudge, don't let me hate. Lord touch my heart. Renew the right spirit in me. I prayed and cried until I fell asleep.

As time went by I still was hurt. I still prayed but I needed more help to get over this, so yes. I seek spiritual counsel. We don't always run to counsel because we do depend on God but faith without work is dead. The Bible says he gives you Pastors after his own heart. People live by a rule of whatever happens in my house stays in my house but not me. Whatever happens here if it's hurting me I'm going to seek help, that's just what I did. I reached out to a spiritual counselor who was willing to help me get through this. I didn't want to go through transition without being healed. Most of the time we transition with no healing and we fall back into the same cycle but this time I wanted to do things

CHAPTER 2: THE ENDURANCE

differently. In order for God to bless and see me through I wanted to get healing.

THE PAIN I ENDURED

Chapter Three
THE CHOICE

After making up my mind, the first thing I immediately did was begin to pray for a fresh start. I wanted to make sure that God sent me the right person to help me through all of this, I wanted to be open but also I wanted to make sure that whatever was in my heart was clear between me and God. I noticed that during that blast of my emotions I had so many spirits I picked up but not intentionally. I had to pray for the spirit of anger, the Bible states in Ephesians that in anger sin not but I did. I prayed for the spirit of jealousy Proverbs speaks on a heart of peace gives life but envy rots the bones. I was beginning to be jealous because all this time all I wanted was to be equal, I wanted to work ministry comfortably, to be accepted for them to see me pushing the vision that was set for the house. Instead things went in the opposite direction. I prayed for the spirit of direction, I learned that I was misguided by my own flesh. The Bible states in Proverbs to lean not to your own understanding in all your ways acknowledge him and he will direct your path. I prayed for my identity and my purpose in him Galatians state that we are the sons of God. I prayed for healing Psalms stated that he heals the broken-hearted and bandage their wounds. I needed God to fix every part of my that ached, that bled, those scars that didn't heal properly. I needed a spiritual surgery done on the inside of me. Last but not least I prayed for a heart of forgiveness. I was reminded with this one on how Peter asked Jesus how many times we forgive and Jesus replied and said seventy times seven. I needed God to forgive me as I forgave them for the things that were done. I didn't want to grow cold and bitter I needed to have a clear clean heart and a renewed spirit. I just needed a down home deliverance for my soul. The first step to deliverance was to acknowledge what was wrong, so I did so in prayer before I knew it God has sent the right person in my life to start the journey of healing the right way.

As counsel begin to take its place I was still having my doubts. In the south we church folks tend to believe that if you leave a ministry something bad would happen to you. You would struggle, get sick or even die and for the longest I had a fear in me that taunted my mind day in and day out about the decision I had made. Lord knows I didn't want to die, struggle

CHAPTER 3: THE CHOICE

harder or to be afflicted with sickness but what do you do when you have been mistreated for so long? Look over. Mishandled. Should you stay and wait on God or do you leave and let God handle the people who done you wrong? I contemplated going back so many times not only because of fear of what could happen but what would they say about me? What would be the new lies they spread? Lord I am scared, I don't want to hear what they say or what they think of me for making this decision. I don't want to have to defend myself and relapse because I have come so far but no matter what has happened to me in that church I still loved and adored everyone there. They had became family to me, it was all I knew and all I wanted. As compared to your real family nobody is perfect but I held everyone close to my heart. I just knew for every lick I took I would one day be able to tell someone my experience and where it got me all because I stayed. I still could but not this way.

During counsel I begin to let it all out. I started from the beginning to the end. Although I have talked about what happened a million times over and over to my husbands and friends, this time it was different, right when I thought I was over it and able to talk about it with no problem, I begin to feel hurt, pain and being mad as if it had just happened. All that matters was that I was releasing it and being able to talk to someone who understood and could counsel me through it. But, Oh man! I thought I was healed, I thought everything was okay but being reminded of the situation hurt. I started to feel empty, cold, out of place and still fighting with

THE PAIN I ENDURED

God about moving on. I wanted to still go back, take my place and just live as if nothing happened. I wanted to feel comfortable again. I didn't want to start over or meet new people it felt like laying on a cold pillow waiting for it to warm up. My heart was sadden and I wanted to just cry. This transition would be new for me and my family. I was stuck between leaving or staying. I knew my season was up, I knew time had left me but I didn't want to accept it. Why now? My flesh isn't ready but my spirit was willing. I knew there was more to God then this but I wanted to transition on my own time but as I was told our time isn't his nor is our ways I had no other choice but to submit to his will. At this point my back was against the wall, all the signs were showing me the answer I had to surrender.

Chapter Four
CLOSURE

I have so many emotions I can't grasp them all at once, with all the questions and emotions I housed I needed a second opinion on my situation. I needed someone or people to see this situation clearly and didn't take sides, and wasn't as involved in church as I was and my counselor. So, I called over my cousins. After an hour my cousins arrived and we begin to talk. I gave them the entire situation and how I felt. I immediately told them I needed them to see this clearly and to be honest no matter how they felt it would affect me. They told me, Sis we never wanted to disrespect your church or knock what you had going on for God because we understood your heart but we have to say for years we wanted you to step back and see this before it came. Most of the

THE PAIN I ENDURED

time we can be too close yet so far that we will miss things or situations that's right under our noses. Each of my cousins told me their experiences just by visiting my church and boy was I hurt. How I couldn't see what they experienced? They expressed to me how their spirit had changed while attending the services and how it made them question what was we condoning. My stomach dropped, I was so shocked. How did I miss it? They also expressed how it took up so much of my time that we barely see each other, how I missed birthdays and family gatherings because I would be swamped with church. How could I explain to them that for the longest we were under the influence of if your family didn't understand why just don't fool with them. If your family thought you were crazy to still even attend the church because of what they didn't understand about the church, just let them be? How could I simply say church divided me and my family? I couldn't say because I was too shocked, hurt and embarrassed. I couldn't put pieces together so I sat in silence and agreed. We all agreed it was officially my time to say goodbye. This had gotten too far. After the intervention, I once again begin to rewind the conversation in my head over and over. I was still in disbelief to what was told to me. Before I knew it all these feelings came rushing at me all at once. I prayed and discussed it over with my husband.

    I begin to ask myself what was the core, root of the issue for me? Why was I still holding on to the pain? Why was I still so upset? Through all these mixed emotions why was I still wanting to hold on to a place

CHAPTER 4: CLOSURE

that was so toxic to me, caused so much pain and why was I so comfortable with wanting to just stay here? My heart still ached. I was torn and hurt by the people there, the people I loved dearly. I had given them my heart and it was ripped apart, my feelings shattered. This was like being in a abusive relationship and wanting to go back because I see the good in the situation and had hope that it would get better. It's so hard to forgive in a situation like this. What do I do next? How do I get up from here? I've confessed, I've prayed but it still hurt. I want them to reap, I want them to feel my pain but I want to be healed and I want to walk away. So, I decided to go back this time I needed closure, forgiveness, peace and liberty.

I have to say during my six weeks of being out during postpartum was tough,things had gotten dark. It has seemed as if everything was going down hill for me. Time was close for me to be back my normal self and work again. I applied for jobs and I wasn't getting accepted. When I finally found a job, I had no baby sitter and my daughter was just to small to be in the care of anyone besides her parents or close loved ones. In this time I feared for my children to be apart from me. My emotions were taking a toll of me, being a mom of not only one but now two kids, managing being a wife was tough on top of trying to really cope and get answers to this situation did I mention the never ending Phone calls, text messages constant reminders of what has happened to us, how the situation ended and how everything we see on social media contradicts what was told to us. Yes, there was still a soft spot there. I didn't want my emotions to get the best of me, I had to be strong but honestly it all was overwhelming. I was longing for a release of my own and not feeling like I was reliving the situation when people brought it up. It was just a constant reminder and all it did was trigger my emotions heavily. I became depressed and even suicidal, not because I wanted to die but because I wanted a way of escape. I didn't want to hear it, see it anymore I just wanted it all to go away. My doctors prescribed me medicine for pain after the birth of my child and I began to find myself taking doses just to sleep. When I would feel myself getting emotional, when I would sit up at night thinking or when my kids would get up early and I wouldn't have enough sleep, I would drown it all out with medications provided to me. I didn't think of it as abuse, I just wanted sleep so I could get an escape, I could get release just for the moment. I was sitting at home during my fifth week of postpartum. My husband came home and he spoke but went straight into the bathroom, I felt like he was running from me. I barely seen him five minutes before he just vanished away in that bathroom seemed for hours. I just wanted a break to think, be alone, breathe. Did he not know I had been with the kids all day? My mind running filled inconsistent thoughts. My emotions just running rapidly. Did he know what I had to deal with all day? People constantly telling me what's happening at this church. People feeding me lies of what they heard or what they thought they knew. Shade being thrower over the

CHAPTER 4: CLOSURE

pulpit pertaining the situation. I was very upset. Once he came out I left the kids on the bed and went into the other room in the dark. I cried. My husband came in asking me was I okay but I wouldn't speak. I was hurt everything was bothering me, everyone around me was a problem and all I wanted to be was alone with myself. The pills were gone and now I was sober there was no way of escaping this time, so everything finally came forth. I had to confess what was the reason I had bursted out the way I did. I told him the thoughts I was having of suicide, how I wanted to escape, I told him I wanted a release and not for my emotions to over take me, I told him how I just felt unwanted, unloved and thrown away from him, the church, everyone. I told him I felt like an announcement board, people constantly pinning the church next move to me as a constant reminder of the situation and even how I'm juggling life being a mom and wife to my family. Lord! I didn't know how bad this was, a simple dose of pain medications became abuse because I wasn't releasing my truth to myself. Yes I was talking but I wasn't healing properly as I should. I was still built up on being strong so no one not even my own family could see me sweat. That night I prayed for forgiveness because of my selfish gain. Instead of giving it over to God like the Bible states in 1 Peter 5:7 cast all your cares on him for he cares for you, I decided to keep them and harbor them thinking I was tough enough to handle my own situation. I am so glad that he cares because I would've been messed up. I understood on this night that God really was keeping me and that he loved me so much he spared me from my own flesh. I am to this day grateful for him sparring my life, what could've been wasn't.

My six weeks are now over and now I am beginning my search for a new place to worship but before I could completely start over I needed closure so I could start new and fresh. The next step I desired a clear heart so I wanted to start by going back to gain peace and forgiveness. When I woke up, I begin to pray ask God for the right spirit and for my heart to be in the right place but as the time got close, flesh crept its way in, I kept playing in my head when I walk through those doors, what will they say to me? How would I react? Would they prophecy to me my next move? Would it be accurate? Is this really my time to go? How do I leave in peace? All these questions were racing through my head all at once but I wouldn't know until I arrive. I have always been nervous when it's time for church because I would have to sing but this time this was another type of nervousness, this was the feeling you get before a big breakup. Here it goes, I arrived to the church and as soon as I walked through the doors I was immediately greeted with an embrace from several members. I can honestly say it felt good after six years of being overlooked, over worked and for the first time ever actually feeling appreciated. I felt like I should have been left for six weeks and came back. I felt loved, even if it was out of their guilt. I came in during praise and worship and I enjoyed the music. During worship I could hear the worship leader and the pastor both exhorting

CHAPTER 4: CLOSURE

pulling and pushing the people to be on one accord for a move of God. Maybe it was me but you shouldn't have to exhort thirty minutes to get God to move especially when it's a desperate need or is in the atmosphere. I couldn't feel his presence and I was reminded of how I use to call on God for him to meet us but the more I pushed, pulled, hollered I couldn't reach him. I would be so numb and empty. People would sit, stare with their heads in the clouds That's the exact familiar feeling I felt. The first thing I wouldn't miss if I wanted to come back. As service continued the pastor gets up with the word and I felt so empty as he begin to preach. I was numb. I didn't feel mad, sad, happy, anything I just felt numb. I felt like there was no reason to hold anything against him because initially I am not God, his judge. I couldn't get upset because I have an understanding that most of the time we all operate under what we have been taught, what's been fed to us for years and we don't know any difference unless it was revealed to us through someone else's eyes. What he understood or thought was no wrong didn't make him wrong technically because nothing has actually been presented to him for his eyes to be open. I couldn't fault him. All I want for him was for him to change his ways and seek God for understanding according to being in leadership and handling different souls. Out of all this I still wanted best for him and the ministry. I couldn't stay the entire service my head hurt and I started to feel disgusted, I felt nausea in my throat. So I got up and left.

Counsel continued, overall I learned that

THE PAIN I ENDURED

becoming angry, bitter, dwelling on the situation wasn't going to change what happen but it could change me. I could miss God being in my own way, wrapped in my own feelings. Though I am the victim I could easily be a suspect to my own situation by my feelings. I learned to hush the voices, hush the thoughts and begin to seek God for his thoughts, his heart, his love, his answers. As time went by I felt more open to this new decision. Day by day I can feel freedom, I can almost see my next level clearly. Though I don't understand fully, my mom always said we would get it by and by. I understand that we can get so comfortable in this spiritual walk with Christ but in order to go higher you have to be put out of your comfort zone to reach higher heights. I understand we are just pilgrims passing through, this isn't our home because of this I finally ready to take the next step, after discussing it over with my husband, I made the decision to join a new church home. I do specifically say the word I because as the situation escalated my husband and I were on separate chapters. I was ending mine while he was beginning one. He was already gone mentally and spiritually but I was still there. He never forced any decision on me but he took his time to be patient with me through the process. He also wanted to make sure I left properly and ended things in the right way.

Chapter Five
I Thought I Was Over It

Sunday morning is here and once again I am nervous. This is the day I join my new church openly but for the first time I'm not dwelling or pondering on what people will say or think. This time I'm nervous because it's a brand new start and here is where all my adjustments kick in. My family and I ate breakfast, prayed and got ready for church. I was excited, honestly I couldn't wait to get there. I knew once I came through those doors Refreshing, prosperities, new life, new fire would be meeting me. When we arrived, we walked through the front doors and exactly what I knew would be there was there. Love, prosperity, life, newness

THE PAIN I ENDURED

was at the door, believe it or not the air was even free and different. I could breathe freely with no hesitation. I didn't have to feel insecure about my clothes. Making sure I was up to part fashionably, making sure my hair was set, making sure my makeup didn't look too bad, making sure that even during praise and worship I looked authentic for the cameras, authentic for the people so they would report back to the pastor, even being authentic for the pastor himself so I wouldn't be ridiculed, making sure I didn't make any sudden moves so people wouldn't get the wrong idea. For the first time I didn't have to worry about the gospel spectators checking me out. Freedom looked and smell good, I never want this to end. My prayers weren't deep, truth be told I didn't even pray like I should but once I came through those doors I knew I was in the right place. Regardless of how far you think you are from God his presence will never leave you. I am a living witness. I haven't felt this in years. It was like starting to date all over again after a rough breakup. Everything new and fresh for a genuine start over. So, praise and worship was going on Then suddenly I begin to shut down. I didn't want to start over. I felt sick and sad fleshly. Why am I feeling this way again? I held my head down to keep my emotions from showing on my face. Once I looked up I seen old members from the other church in the congregation. I got so upset, I felt hurt all over again. I was irritated. I didn't want to join anymore, I knew I should have went somewhere nobody knew me. I knew I should have stayed out of church. I really wasn't ready,

CHAPTER 5: I THOUGHT I WAS OVER IT

I am once again just mad. Ugh! When will all this be over? I know they say don't be in your feelings regarding ministry because your feelings will be hurt. Too late, I was already overtaken. Our city was just way to small I vote for us to move, another state, another country would be even more pleasant then sitting here seeing these people again. They say the devil be in church and I NEVER believed it until I encountered these people. Why are they here? Leadership has always been on their side, they always had the upper hand. Why do they follow me at a new place? The devil did it this time he sent such a distraction to throw me completely off and it almost worked.

    Here we go, though I don't want to do it I stepped out on obedience and faith. Regardless of what I feel I decided to join anyway. Obedience is better then sacrifice. At this point I wanted healing and I wanted it bad so even if doing this would cause for me to get it, I'll silence the opinions, the noise of the people and do it. After service so many of the members came and embraced me, I felt that this was the right move even while feeling still. Everyone was so happy, many said they were waiting on us. I felt good. After service we all returned home and I was feeling good. Tuesday morning came and I got up to fix breakfast for my family and immediately I heard the lord say the curse is broken. I will be honest, I shoved it off and I second guess myself because I didn't think I heard what I heard. Suddenly I heard it again: "The curse is broken." I took heed to it and went about my day. As night grew I begin to get my kids

THE PAIN I ENDURED

ready so we could attend our first night of word study at our new church. Boy was I excited, I had my bible and notebook ready. Once my husband arrived we were all on our way. We came late, I was so itchy to get inside. When I came in the Pastor was speaking on curses being broken over our lives and how we had to denounce them. I was reminded of what I heard the lord speak earlier that day, I received every part of it. Service was getting good, I looked up and I seen the member again and immediately I started battling in my mind. Why are they here? Why did they follow me? I made up in my mind I wasn't coming back. Six years of pure silence while getting harassed, bullied, lied on I don't want to repeat this cycle. Lord am I bitter, envious, angry? Am I harvesting things and beginning to become toxic? I need to look in the mirror and analyze myself. I spoke with my counselor and cleared my mind on this situation. I couldn't quit, I couldn't walk out, I had no escape. I knew someone depended on me, I knew ministry was on the inside of me but I needed God to get me through this. So I made a decision to detox, take it old school. I decided to fast and pray.

Every morning, during my time of detoxing (fasting and praying) I declared in the atmosphere that God was a healer, I read my daily devotions, I prayed for my heart and I declared that I was forgiven and so was the people who has done me wrong. I meditated, prayed, rest and things started to come along. Tuesday night came and it was finally bible study time. Once six o'clock came I rushed and got everyone ready so we

CHAPTER 5: I THOUGHT I WAS OVER IT

could all be on time to get our spiritual food. While attending bible study I paid close attention to what the pastor was teaching. The lesson was based on being the light and Godly love. What stuck out to me most was loving people who misused you and being able to speak and pray for them without being seen and doing things whole heartedly not based on what was done. I was convicted immediately on my spirit. I asked God to forgive me, then I did what I should have done in the first place, I confronted my emotions from judgment, abandonment, rejection, pain, envy, jealousy. I went to the source to get the answers I needed so my healing process could be complete. I received the answers that I needed and immediately peace embraced me, I was so free at the same time I also seen where I was selfish in this time of hurt because I was so stuck on me being victimized that I didn't even include or consider anyone else's feelings. I asked for sincere forgiveness, here is where I found closure. I kept telling God thanks because I finally could see, I wasn't blinded anymore. I was ready to clean up the blood, to be sewed up and stitched and to heal properly. I could feel again.

A week later, I had to start over as a babe in Christ after asking for forgiveness and being able to heal properly I rededicated my life over to Christ, started back reading and studying the bible, and praying. Day by day I found love for ministry again, the fire rekindled on the inside of me. I was refreshed. I was a new creature. I had let everything go and I was ready to over new. I continued to go to church and hear the word honestly day by day things came together. I notice I was going days without even noticing anything about the incident that took place, I wasn't thinking or talking about the church, I wasn't reminiscing, I wasn't forcing myself backwards.

One night surprisingly, my friend and I went to eat. As we laughed and joked we walked in, we settled down to wait and be seated. Here was the test, I glanced up and seen my old leadership, I immediately looked away. I wasn't nervous, sad or mad I was just surprised. I sat watching the waitress prepare our table, while doing so in my peripheral I seen him walk towards me. I stood and I greeted him with a hug. As I continue to look pass him I saw his parents, who use to be my spiritual leaders-overseers, I waited for them to approach me also because usually they always ran me down to speak and never missed a beat, so I expected that this time also. I was shook who knew I would see the day the man I called my spiritual father couldn't look at me in my face. He and the woman I called spiritual mother walked out the door with their head down. I didn't know what to do, or how to respond. I just sat there staring straight ahead, I was thinking this couldn't be right. You are the man of the cloth, you preach and teach about the contradictions of loving God and not speaking to people. I told my friend is this really happening right now? I was shocked and honestly that hurt my feelings. Though we may haven't agreed I expected us to be adults. He use to call me daughter, was anything he said true? A real father never looses love or stop fathering a child due to

CHAPTER 5: I THOUGHT I WAS OVER IT

their difference. I guess God's will isn't what I preferred but I am free indeed. I did my part.

So I wasn't operating in ministry I didn't even sing because I wanted to start completely over and new this continued for another month. Finally, I felt the spark to begin singing on the praise team. My first day of practice I wanted to back up completely, I was nervous, although I was willing I was still registering the structure I once knew. Everyone welcomed me with open arms and although it wasn't what I was use to I felt good to rehearse with open spirits, open minded and God fearing people. I could be myself and not on egg shells and however the Holy Spirit lead me, I was sure that everyone had my back. I introduced them to a brand new me. I was ready to take the world over and give them a gift a man named Jesus.

THE PAIN I ENDURED

Chapter Six
I OVERCAME

Sunday came, after the rehearsals it was time to go forth. Yes I felt free and felt good but I completely backed out. I once again didn't have the confidence to be back with a new group of people. My mind kept me captive, I thought this battle was over but In the midst of this my mind introduced me to depression. I was breaking down with a smile on my face. I just wanted this to go away fully, I wanted something new but I didn't like the feeling of it. It felt uncomfortable like a cold wind. I was free but my mind wasn't. I had to deal with my mind it kept second guessing me, tricking me into thinking that I wasn't ready, that I couldn't do it. So I went back into prayer once again to capture my mind and free it from captivity. I made a decision not to go back to church, to detoxed again. My mental health had to be watched, I was struck with fear once again. This time I had the right tools to fight. I begin to pray and declare over my life what God has done for me and how I won't be defeated again. I went into prayer a cub and came out the next morning a full lion. I shall not be defeated. My mind was made up, I got back up and tried again. When it started to feel uncomfortable I pushed through and before I knew it was ministry again but this time like a mad woman.

    Yes I've had my ups and downs and will continue with the job of ministry. The story of ministry never ends, there will more that I will face but as long as I have God Deuteronomy 31:6 who will never leave or forsake me, Philippians 4:13 I will be able to conquer anything with him.

About The Author

Psalmist Jessica Beckum is a wife and mother of two beautiful children. She is an upcoming gospel artist and a worshipper at heart. Through many trials and circumstances she has proven her strength and tenacity through Christ to overcome. Her ministry move far beyond generations, she has been called to impact generations in her own unique way.

www.ingramcontent.com/pod-product-compliance
Lightning Source LLC
Chambersburg PA
CBHW021124080526
44587CB00010B/635